FIREWORK COLORING BOOK

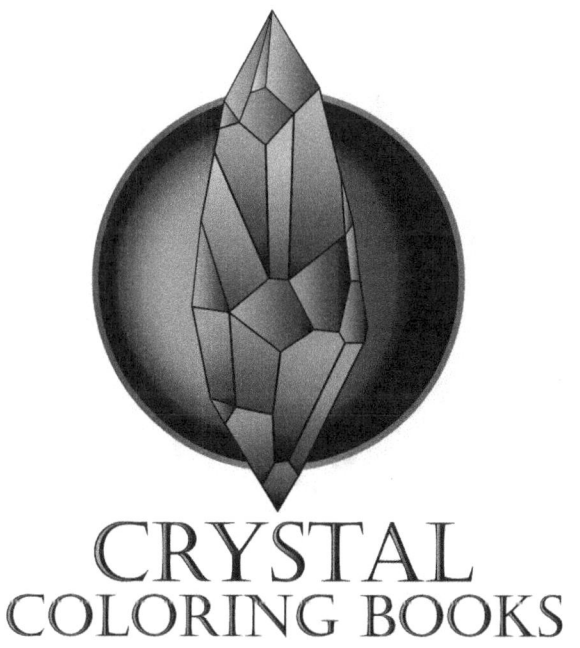

CRYSTAL
COLORING BOOKS

Copyright © 2017 Crystal Coloring Books
All rights reserved.
ISBN-13:978-1978471771
ISBN-10:1978471777

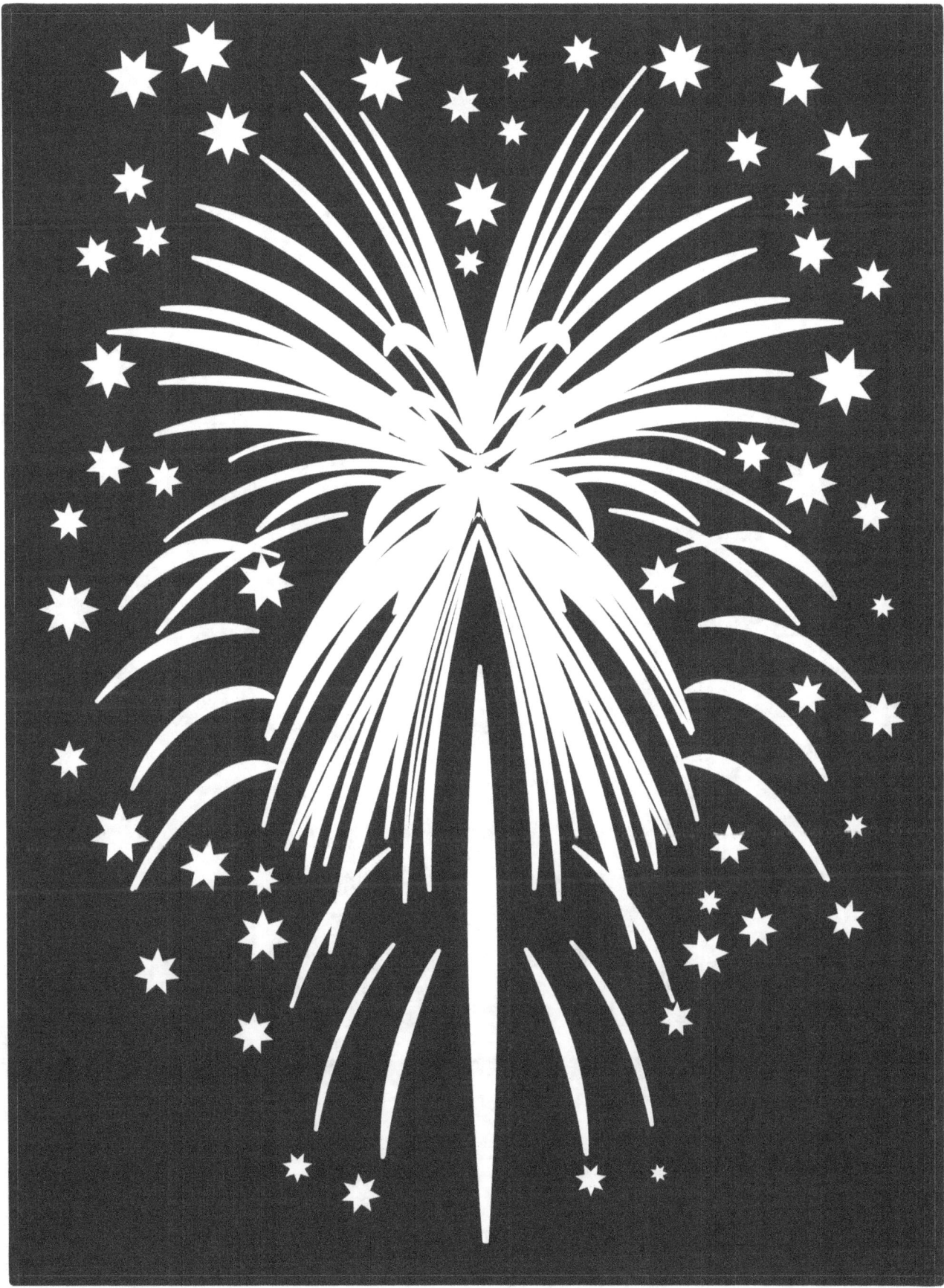

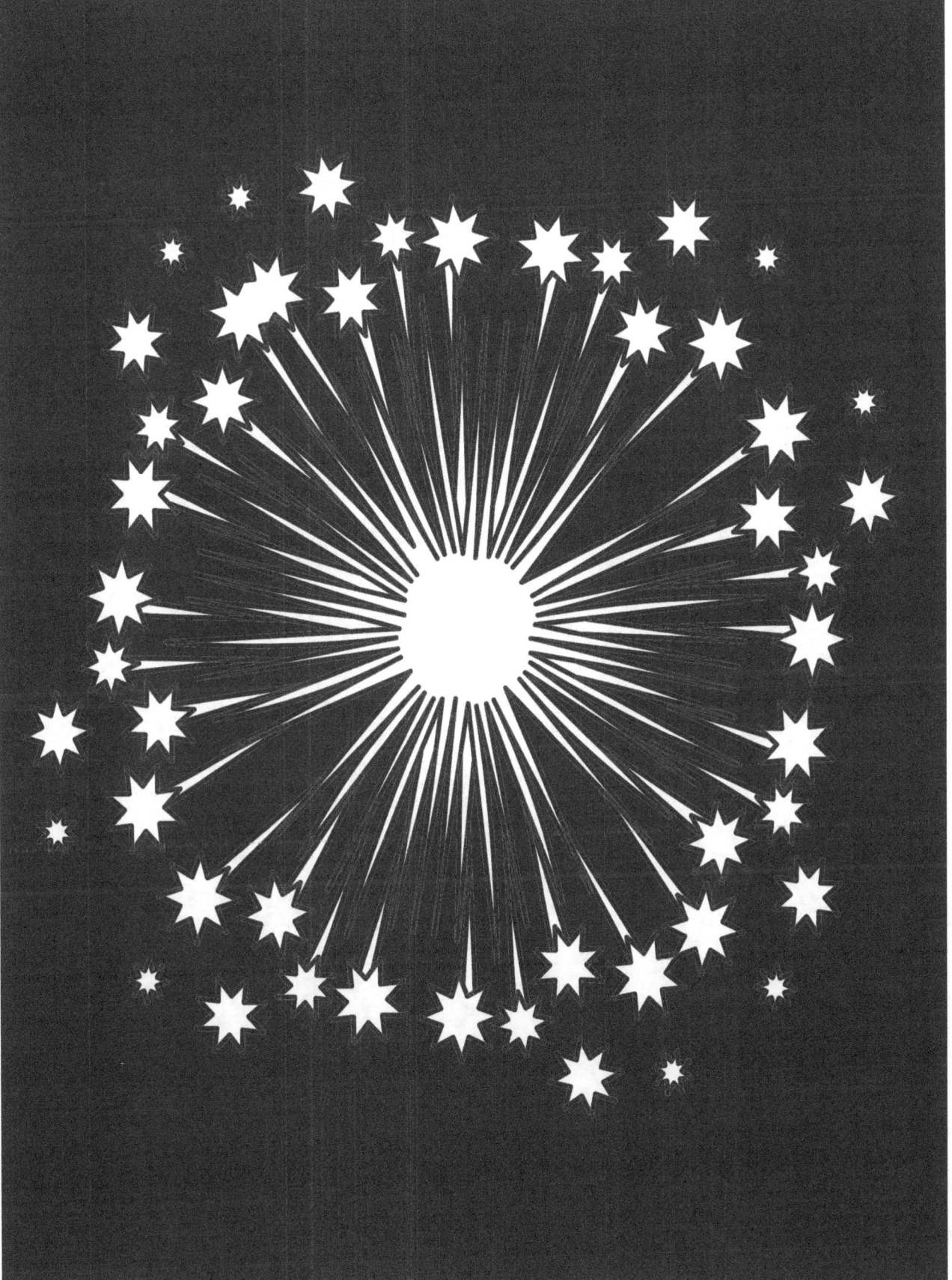

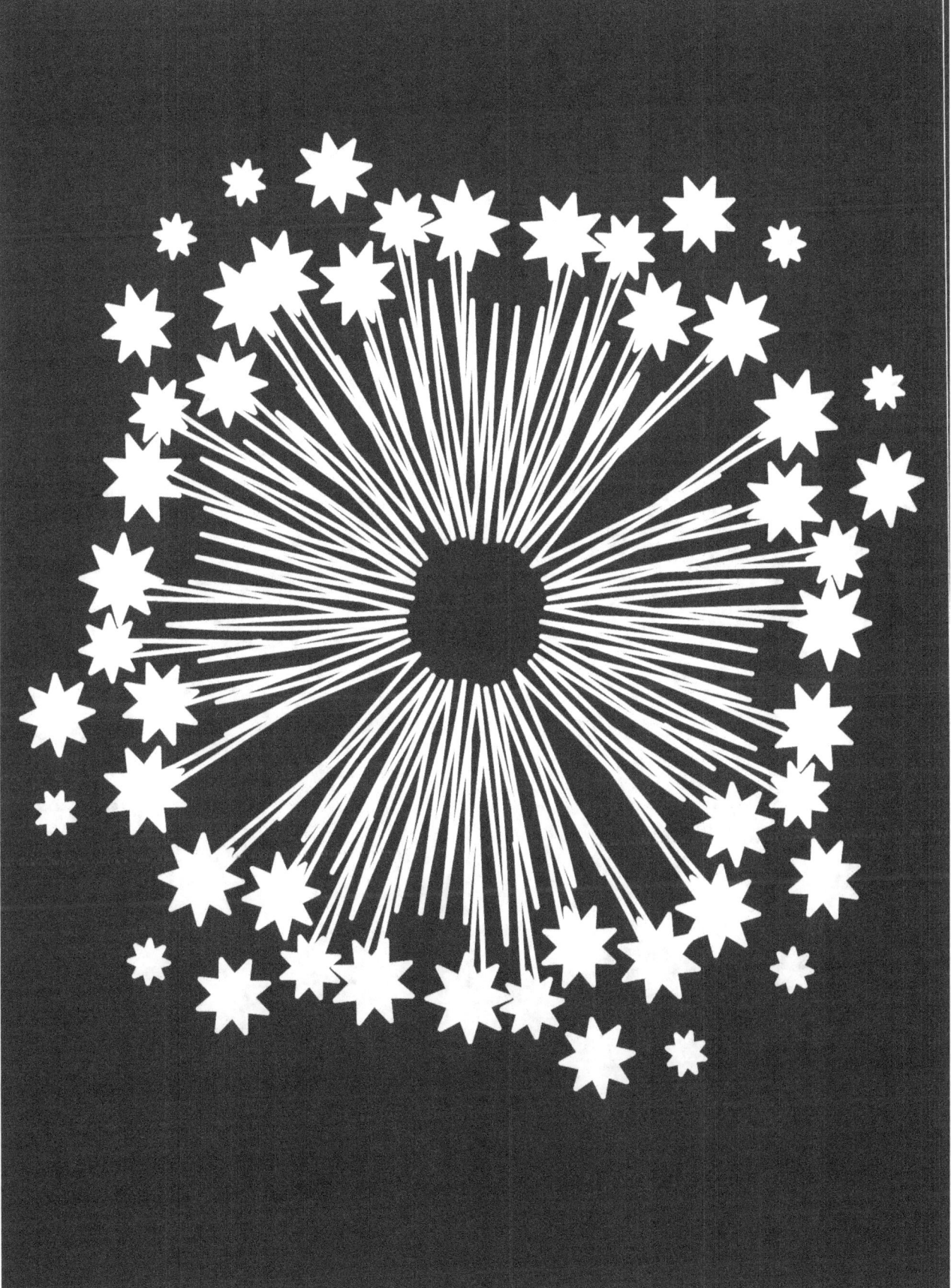

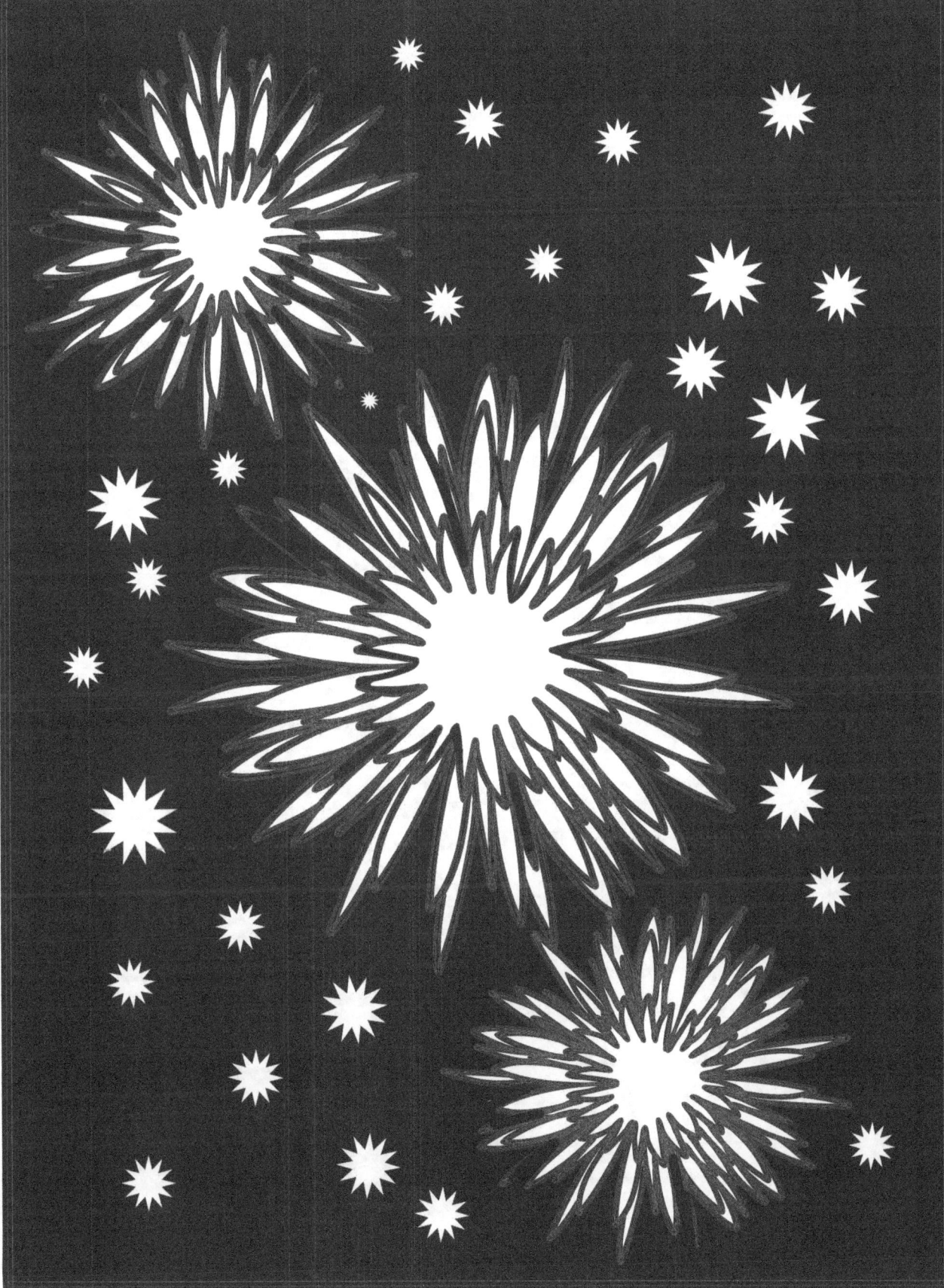

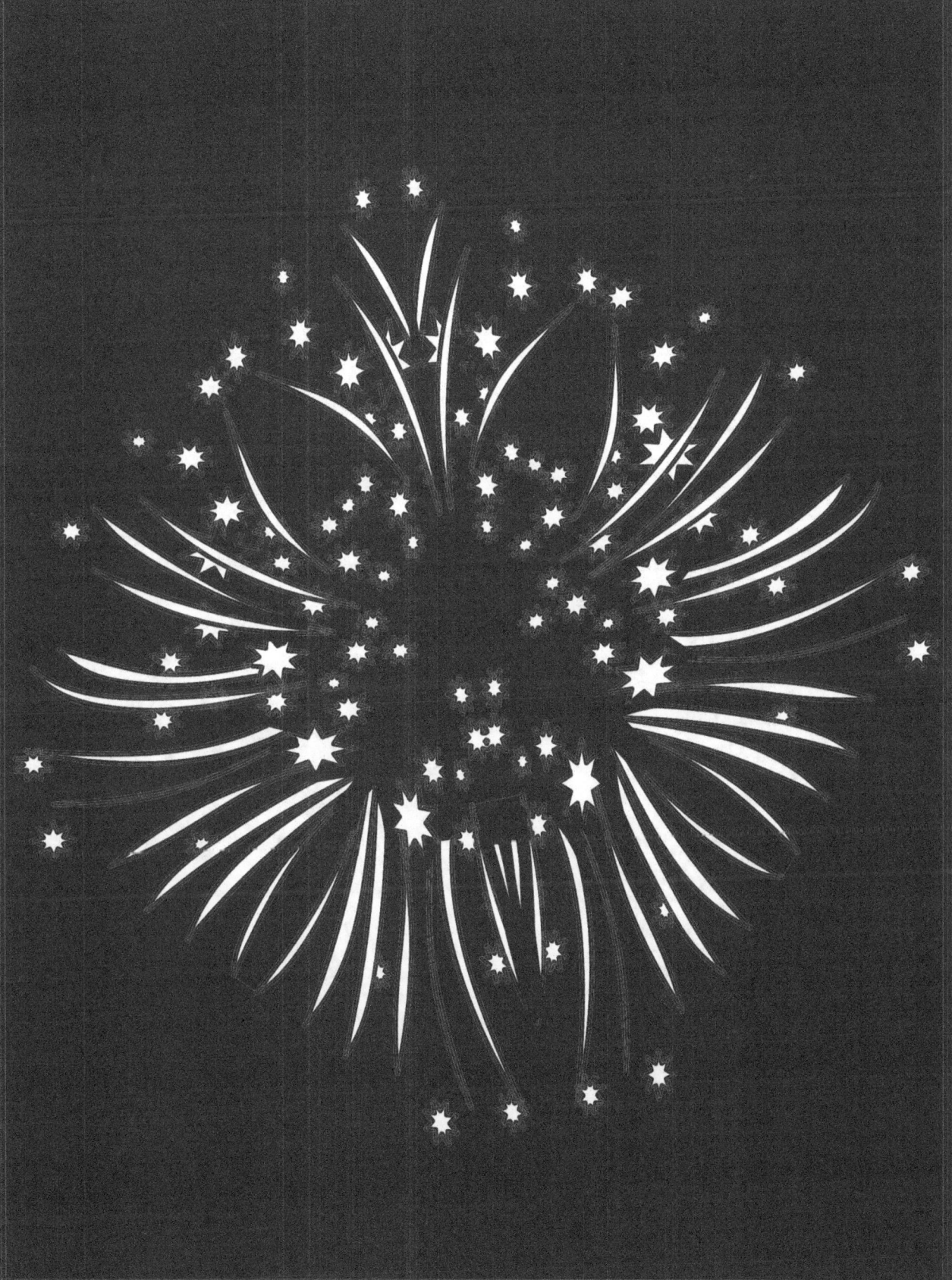

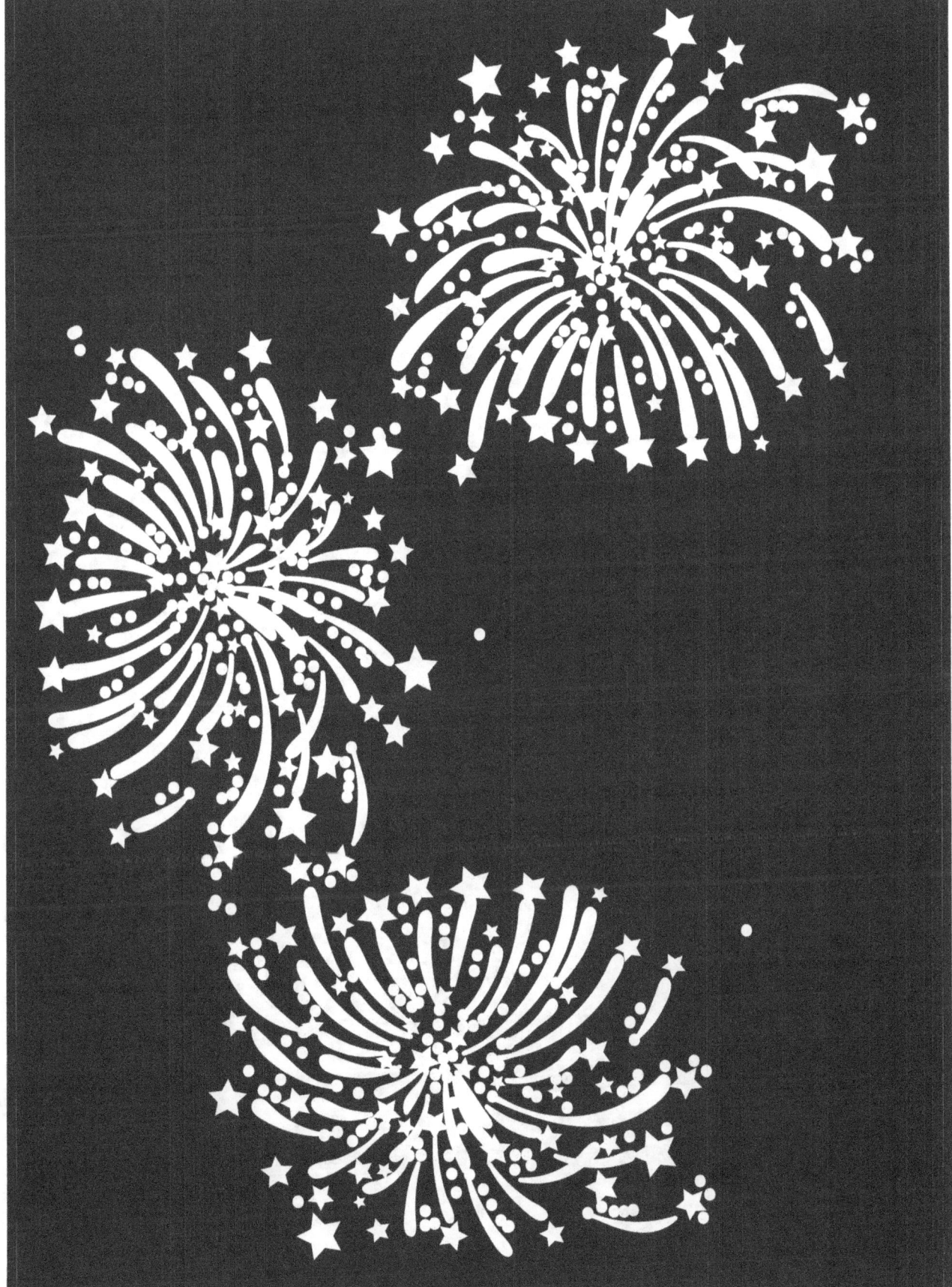

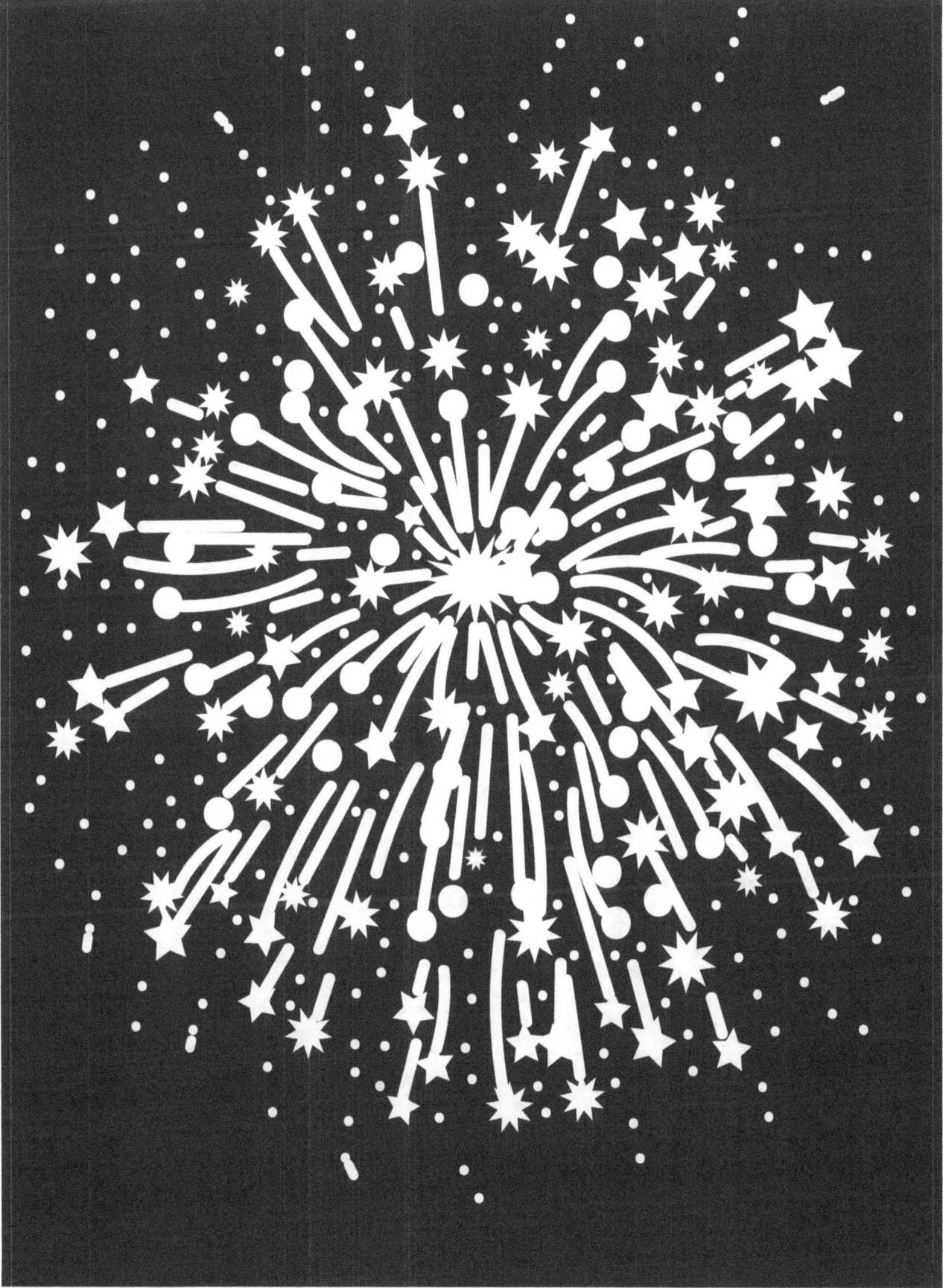

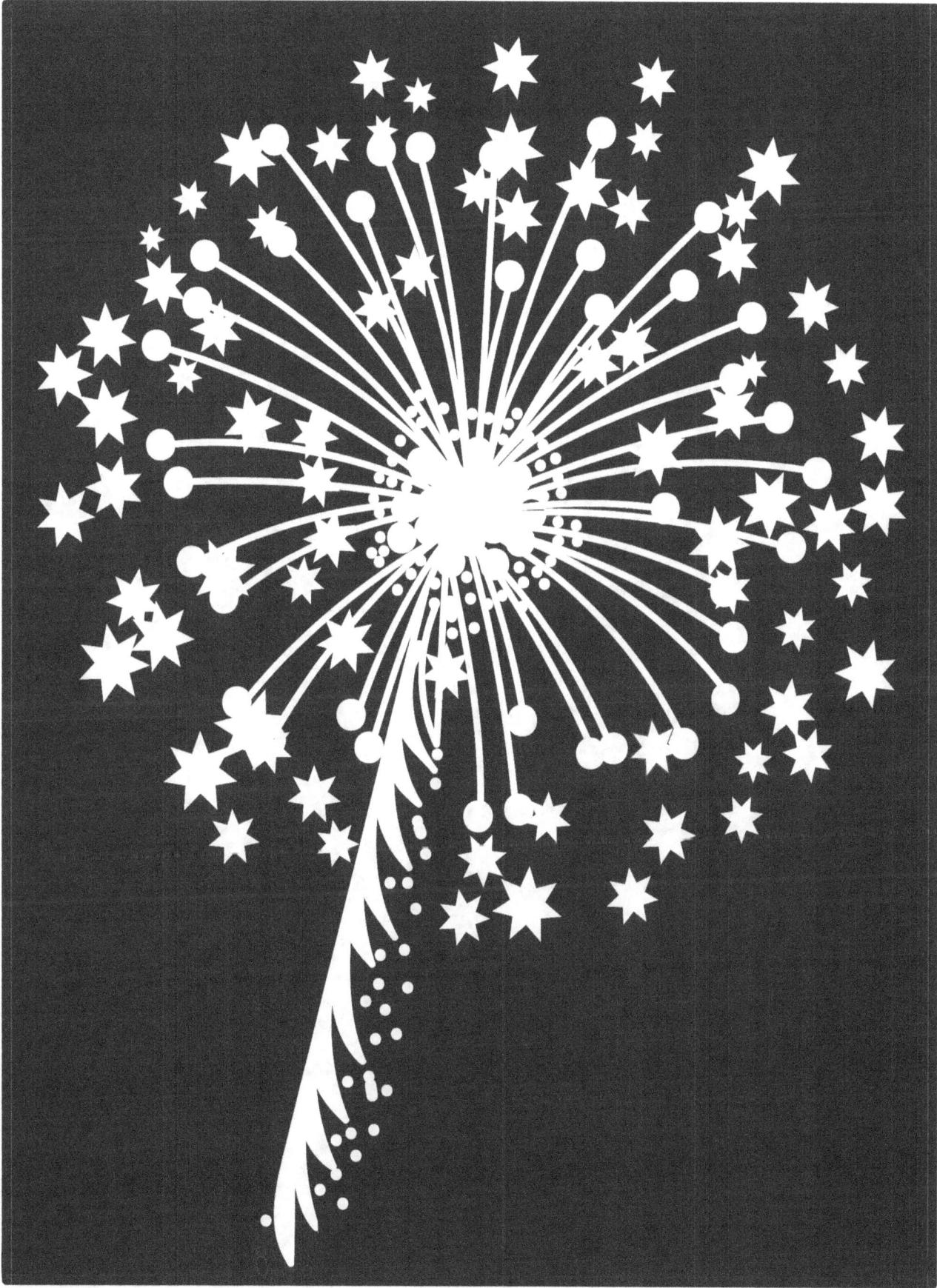

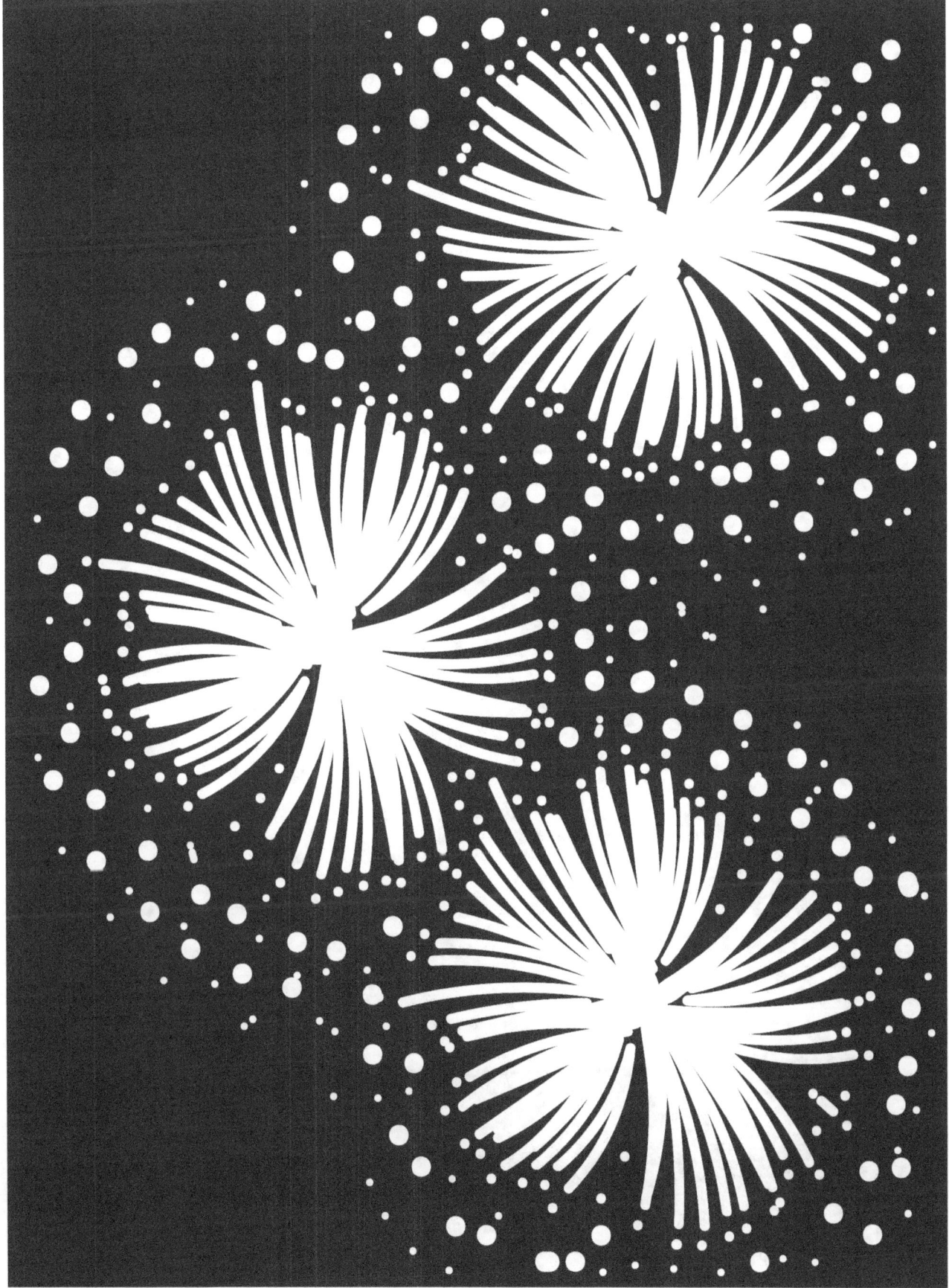

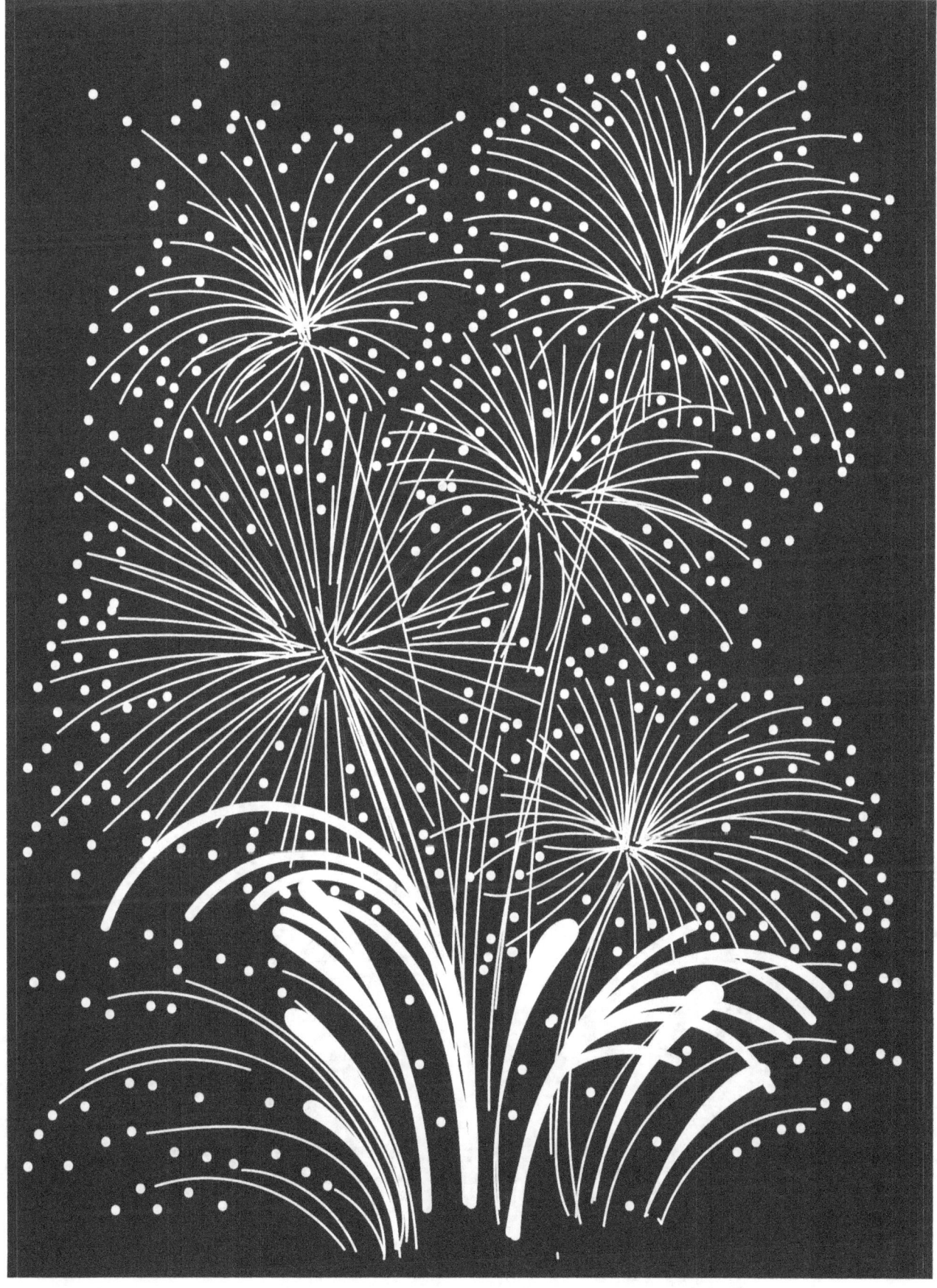

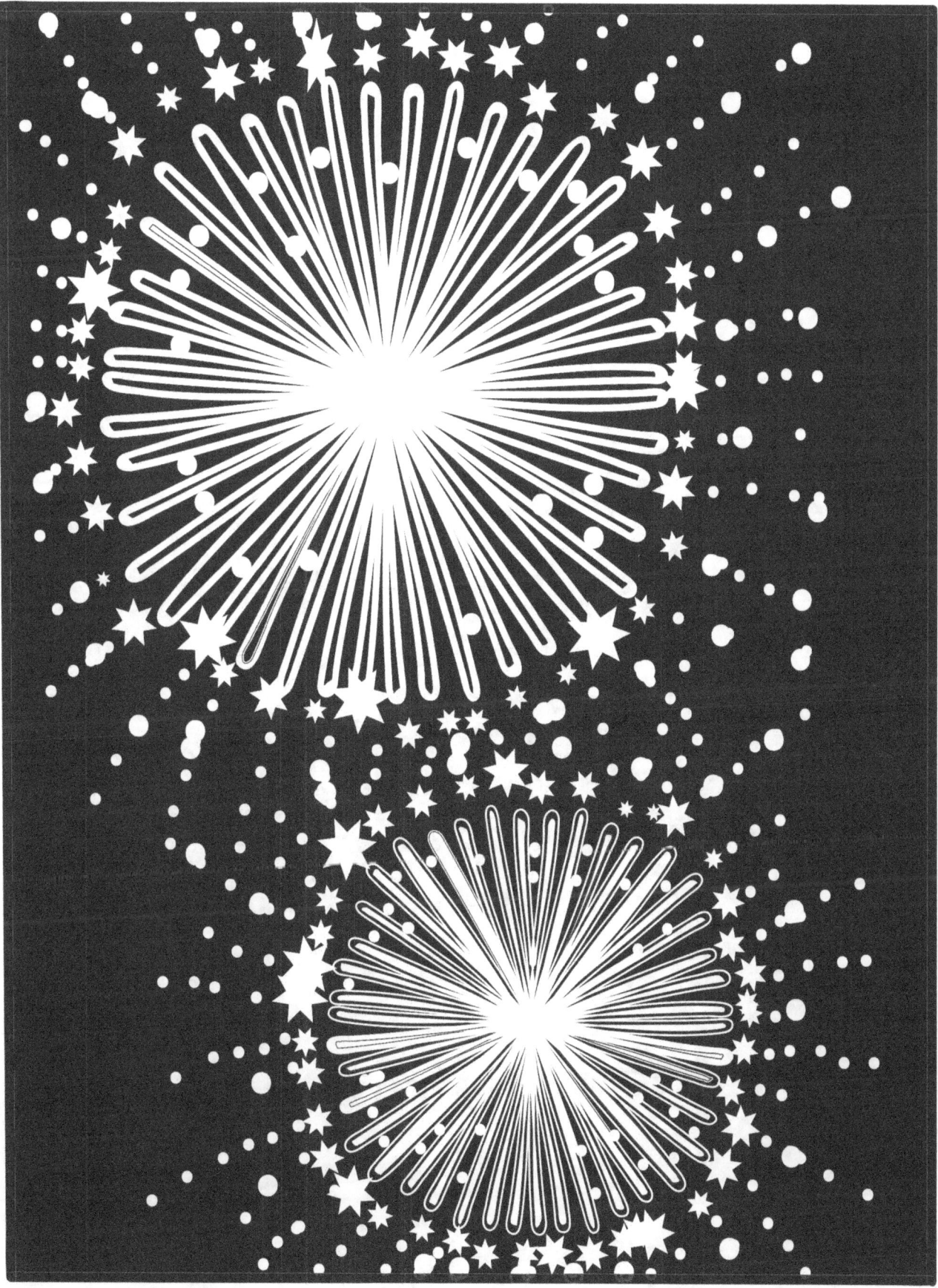

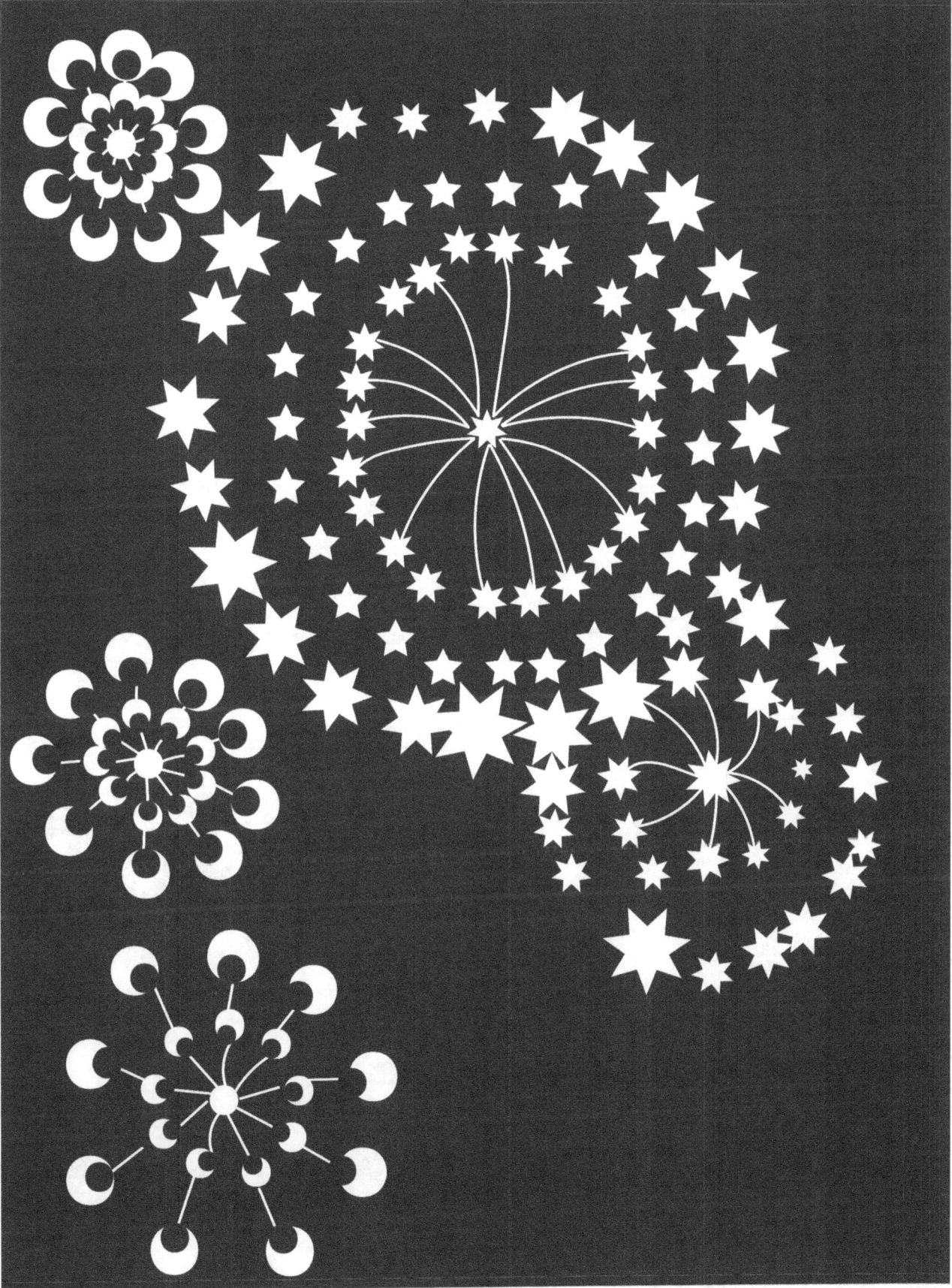

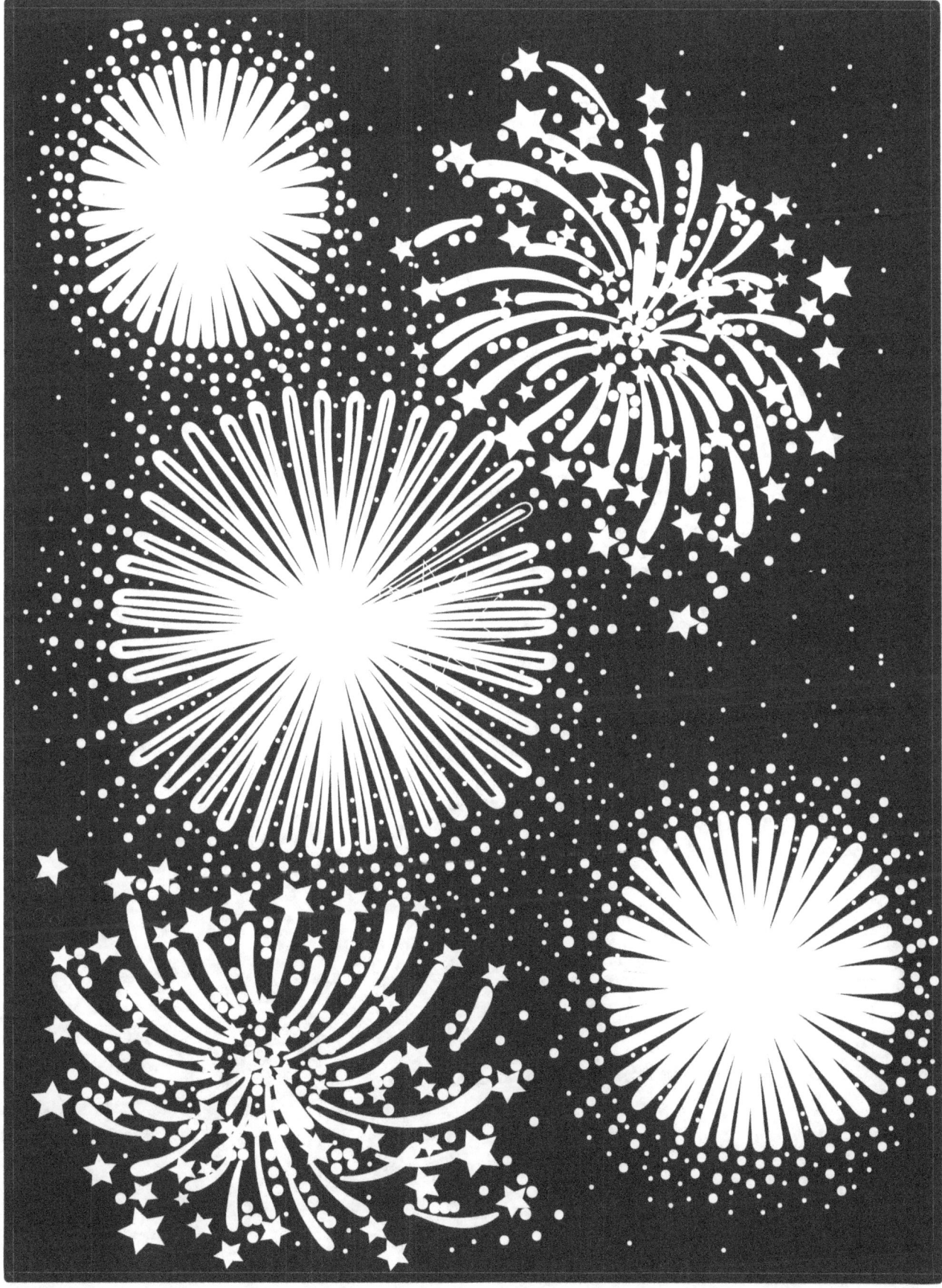

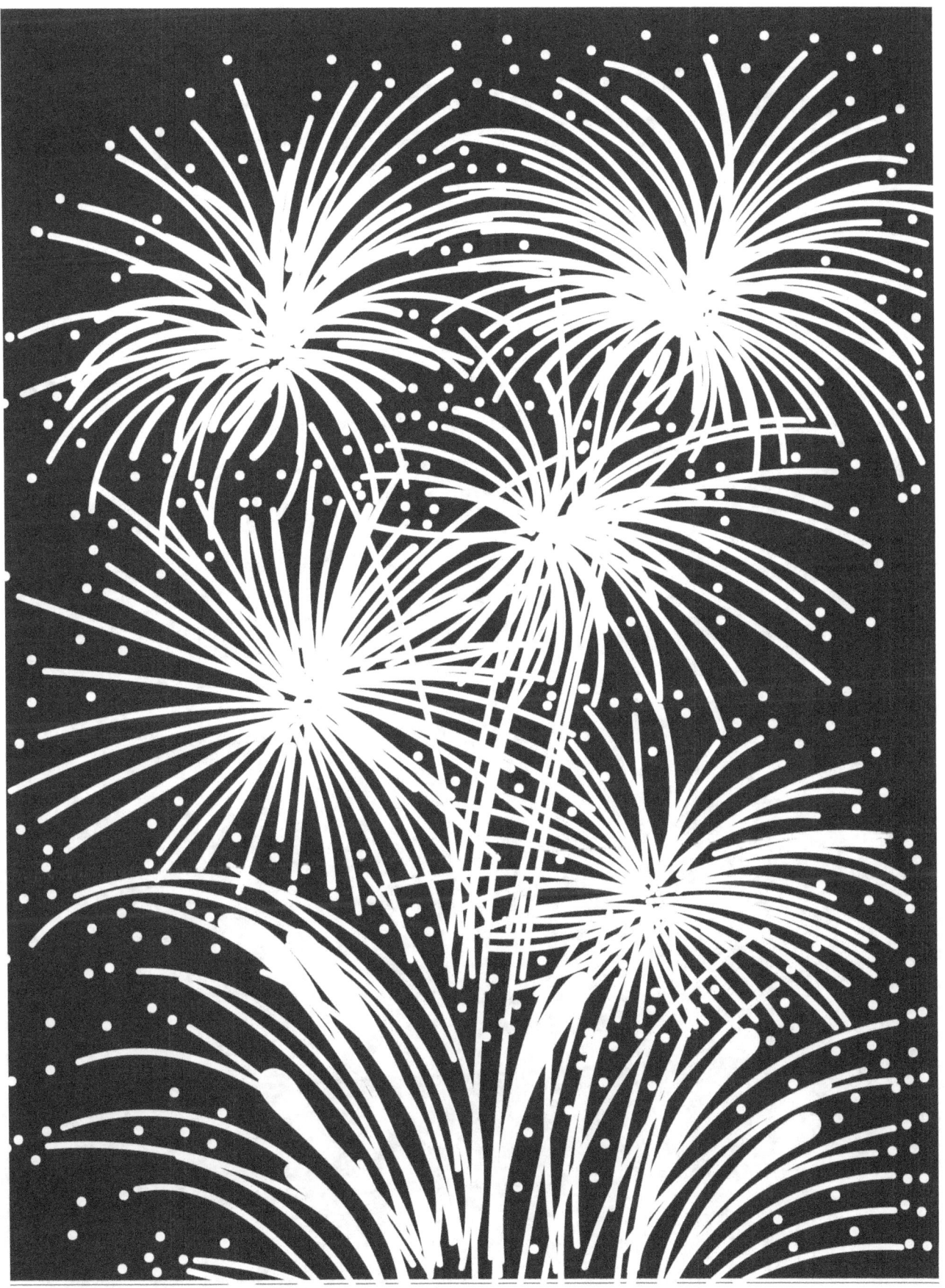

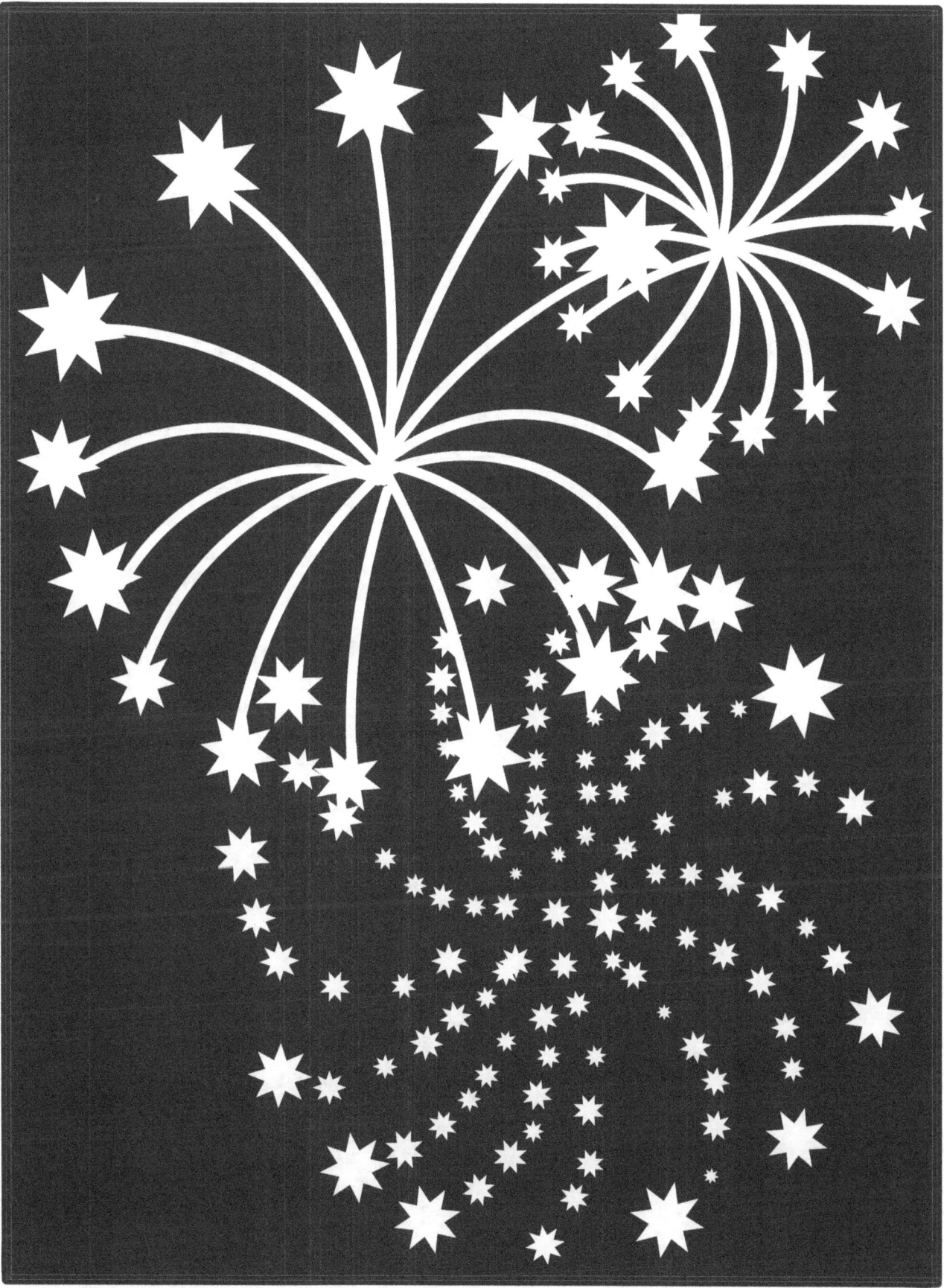

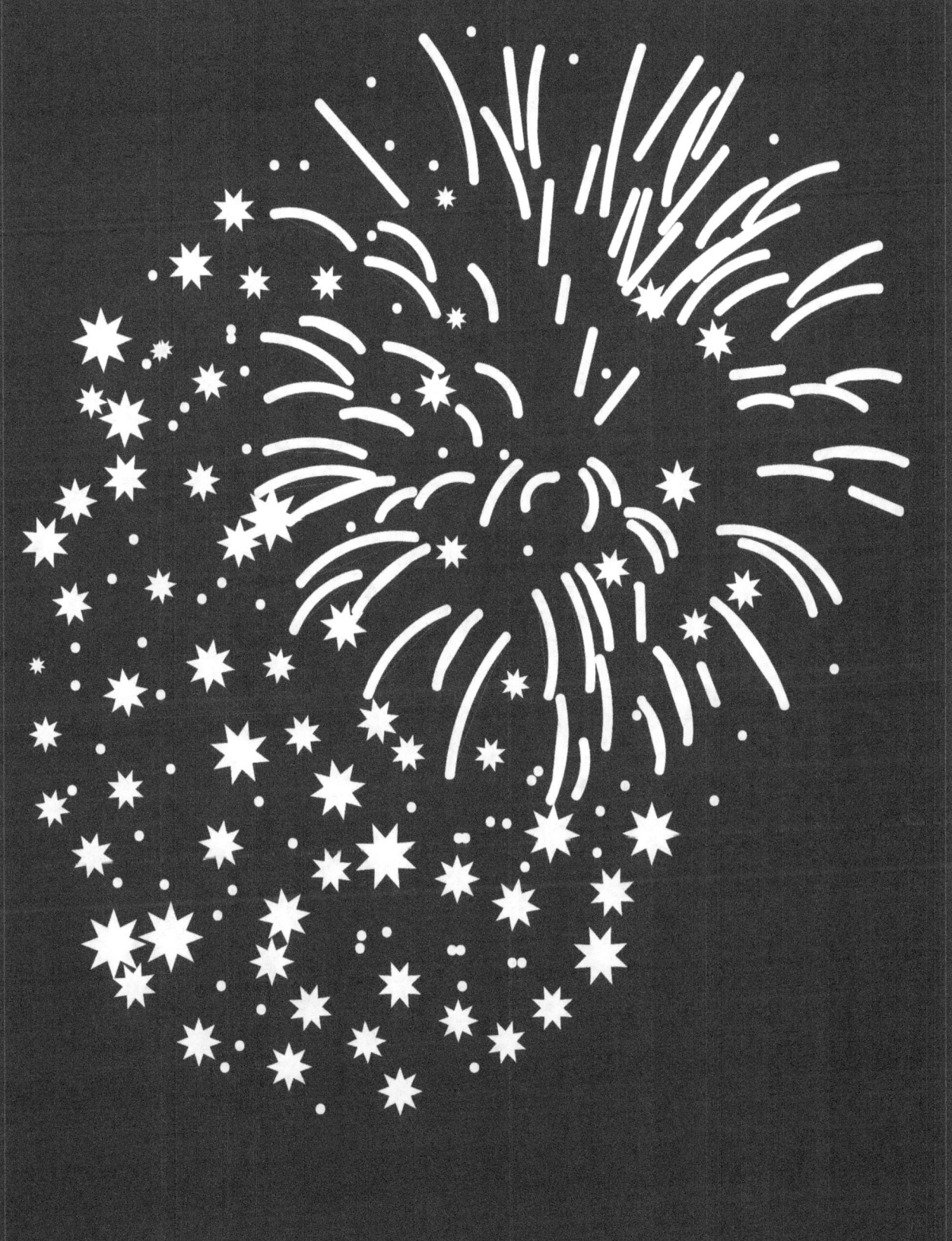

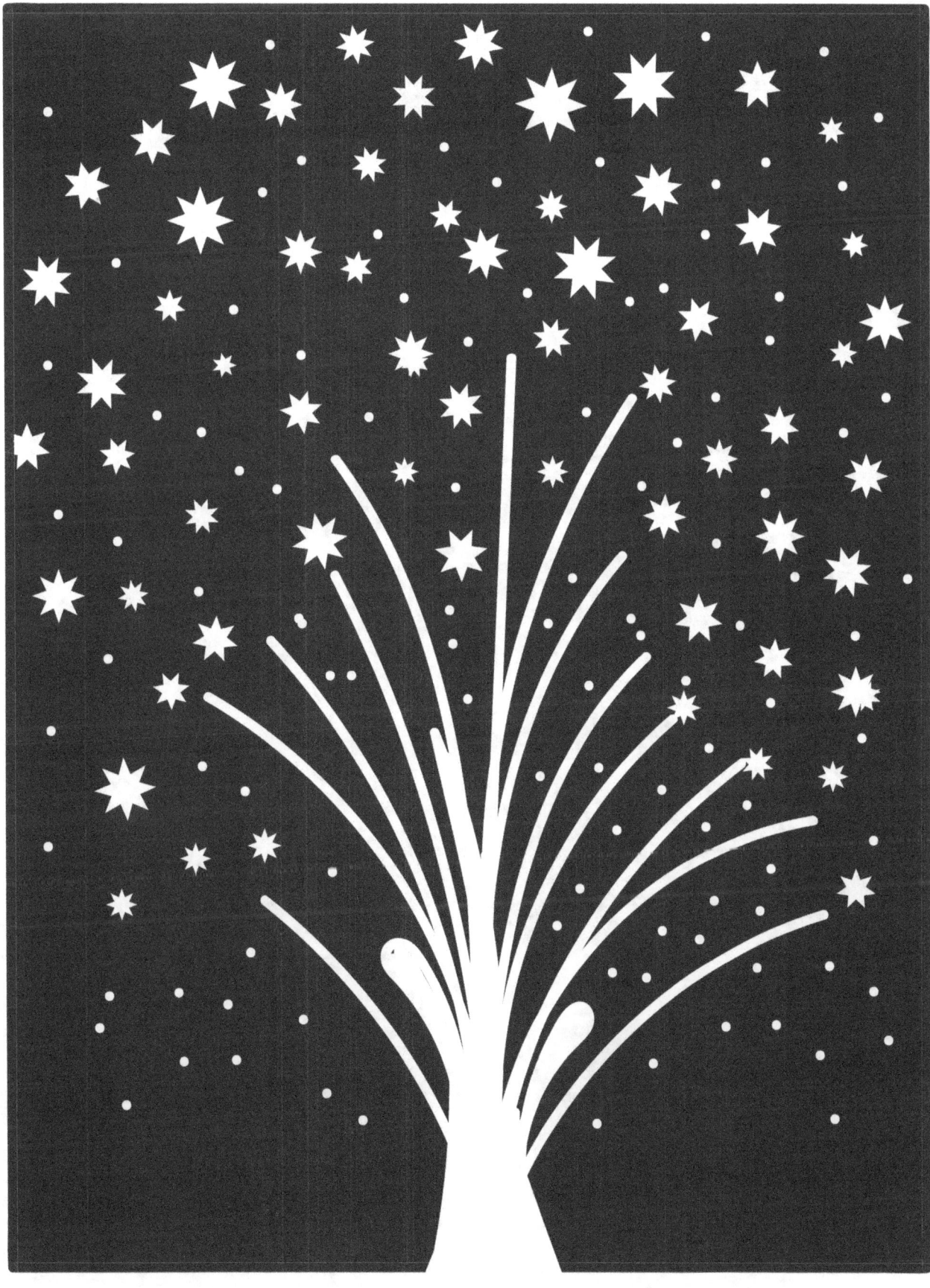

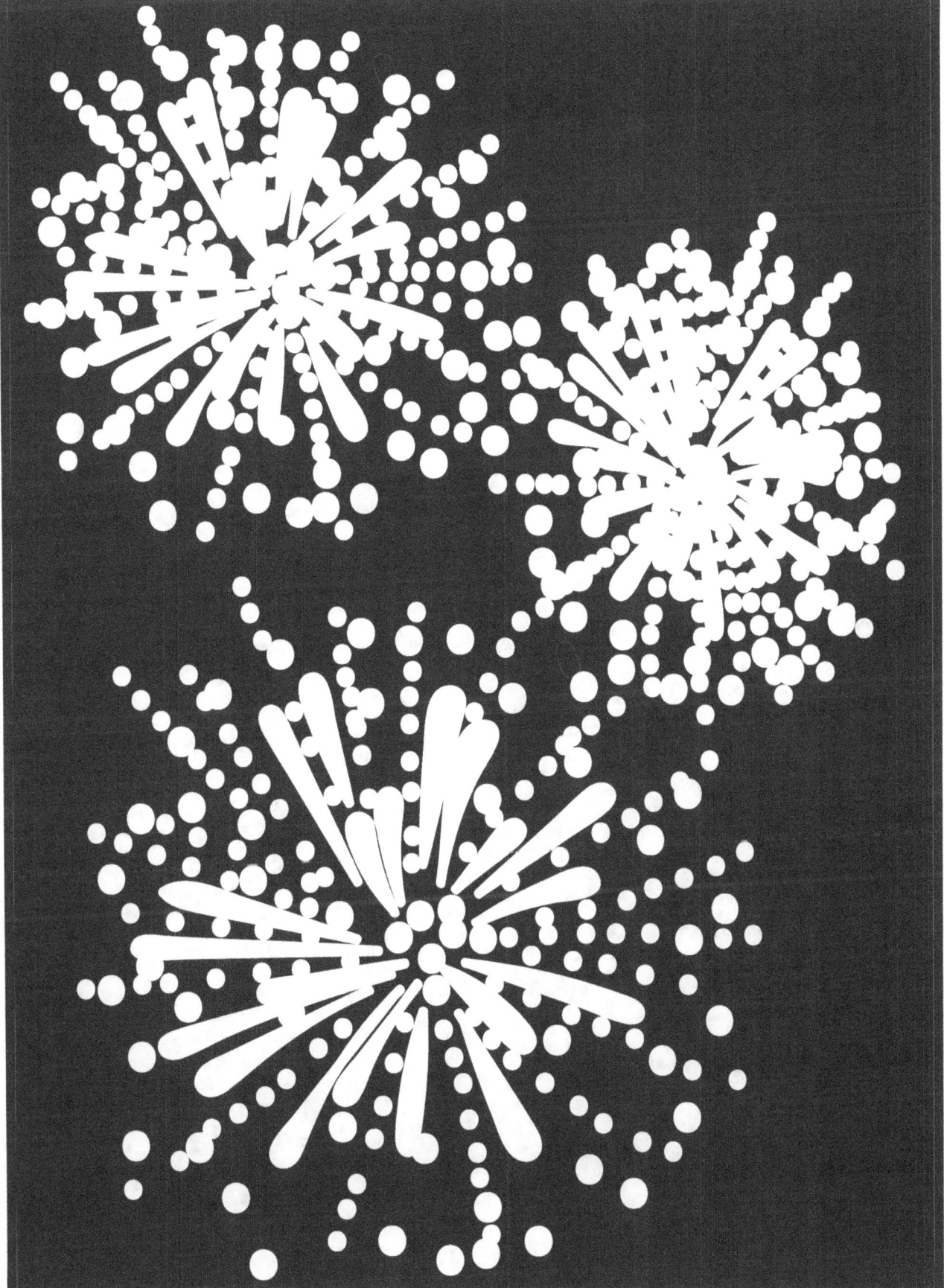

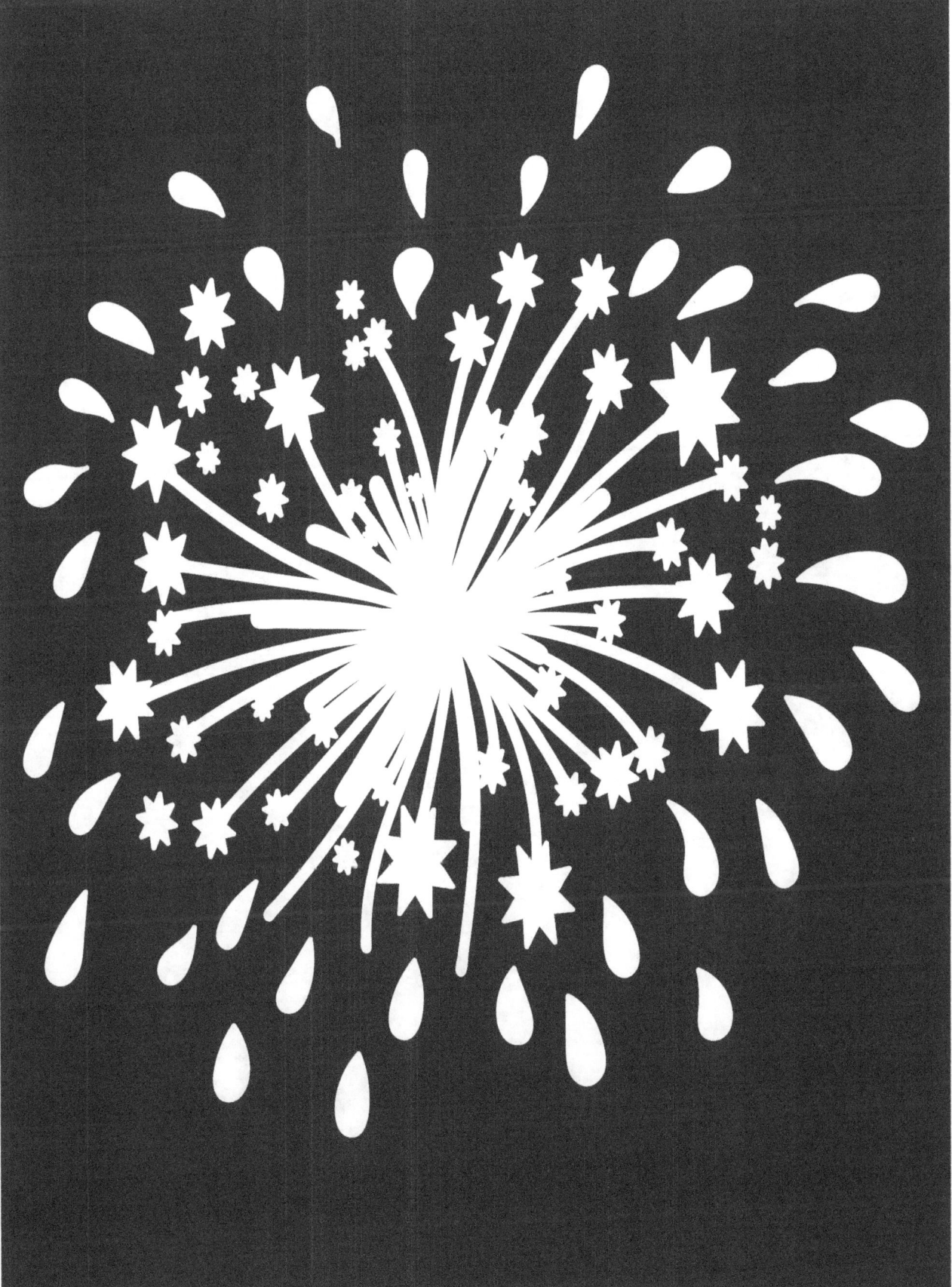

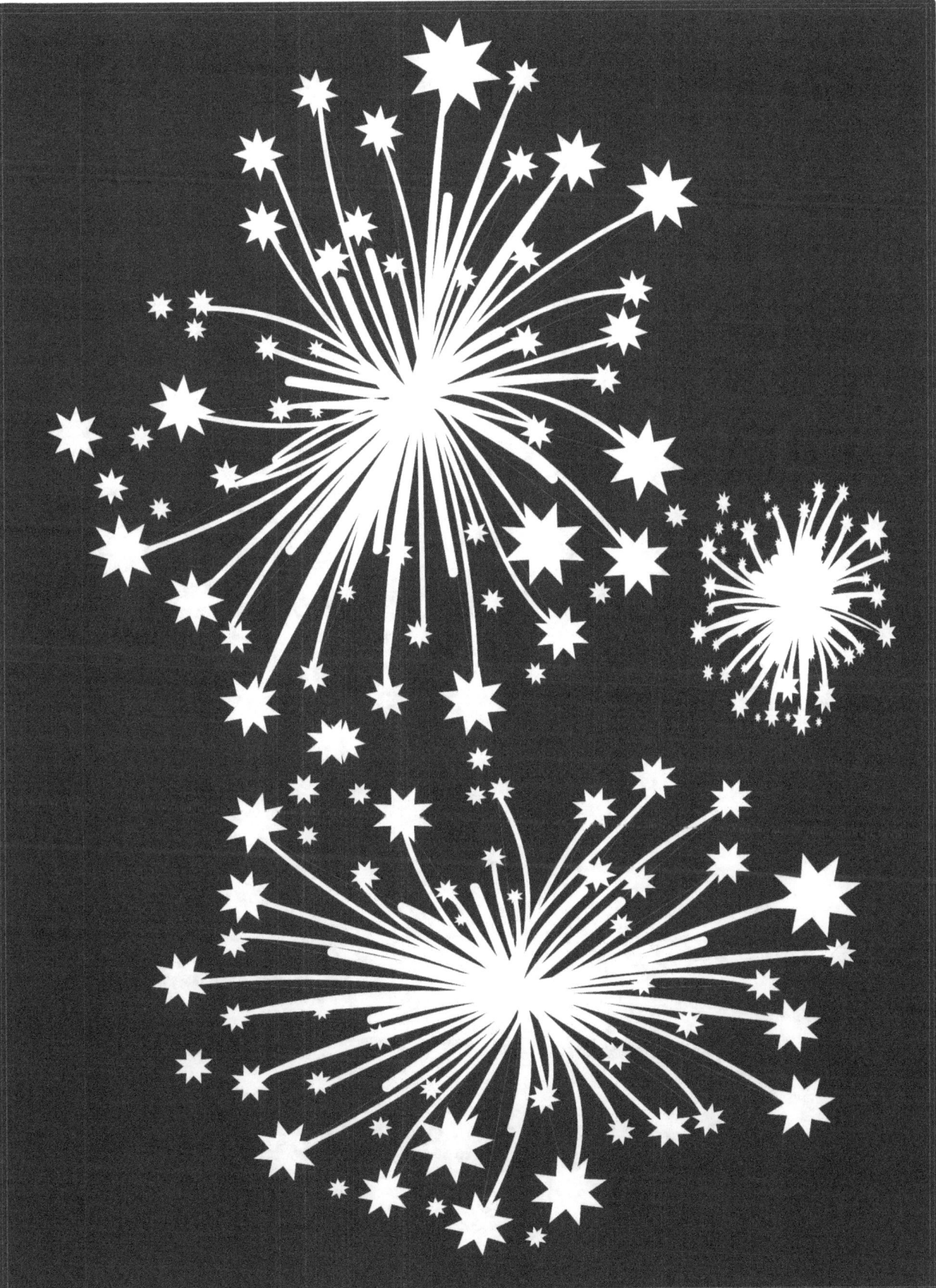

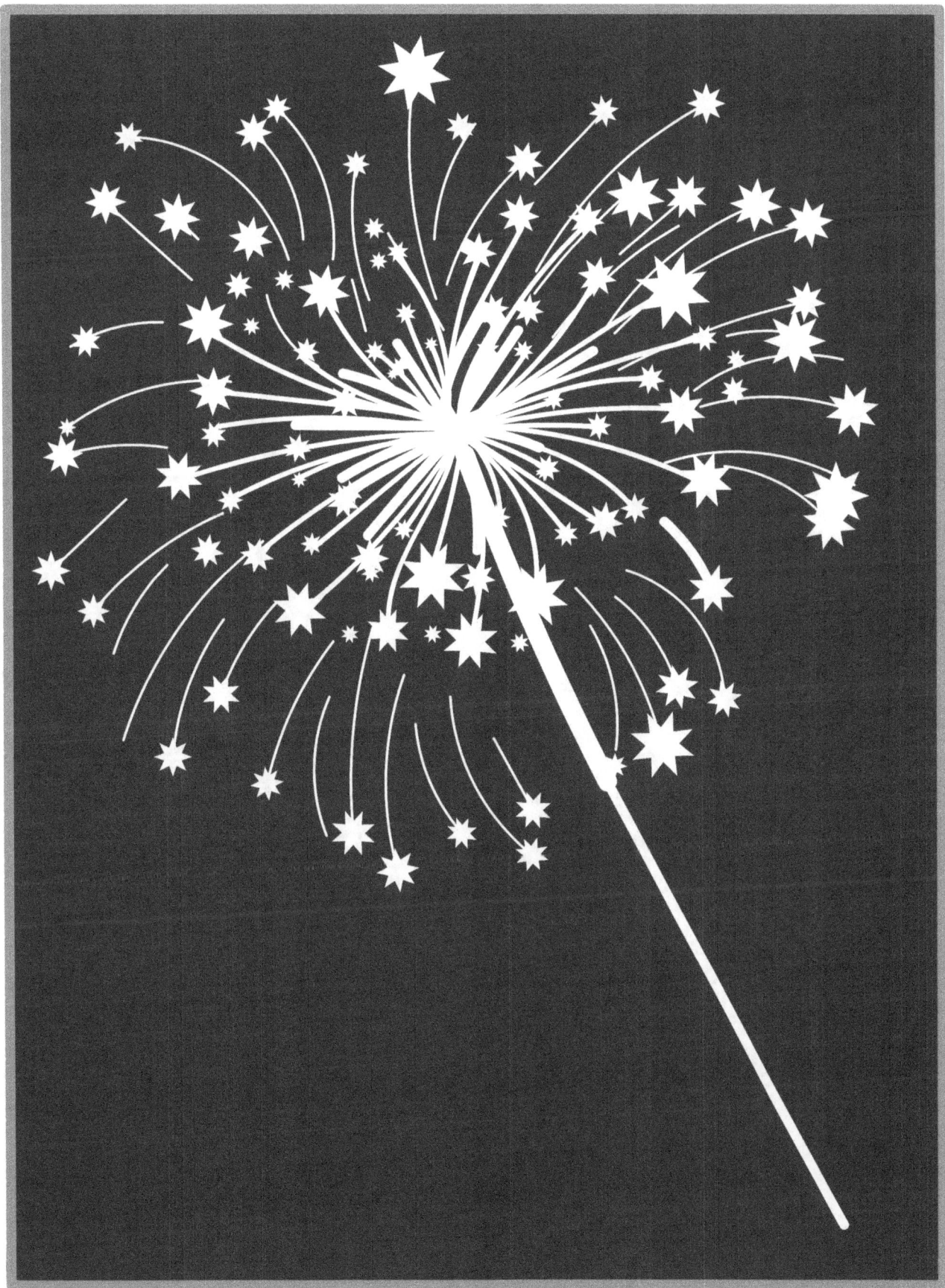

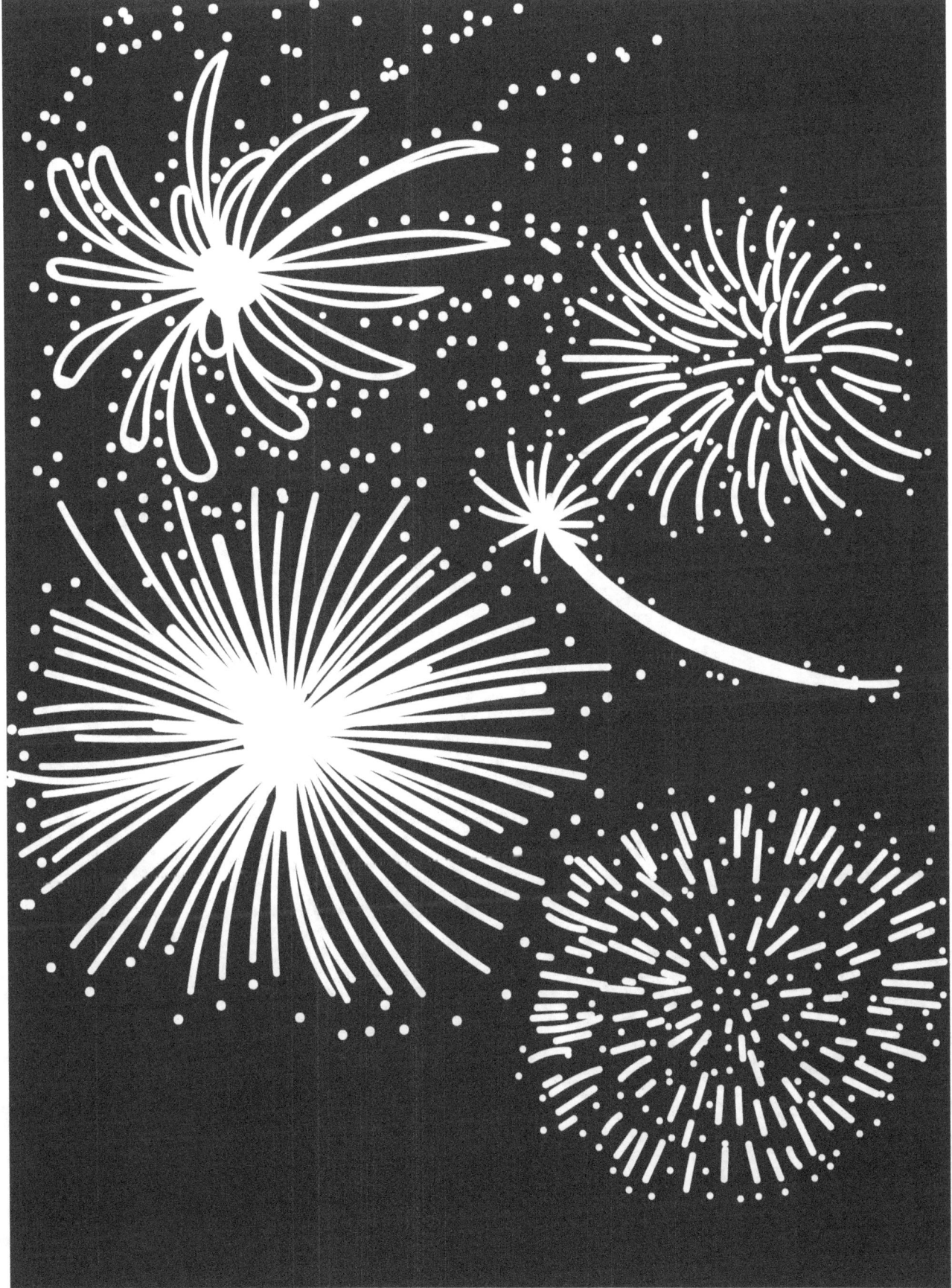

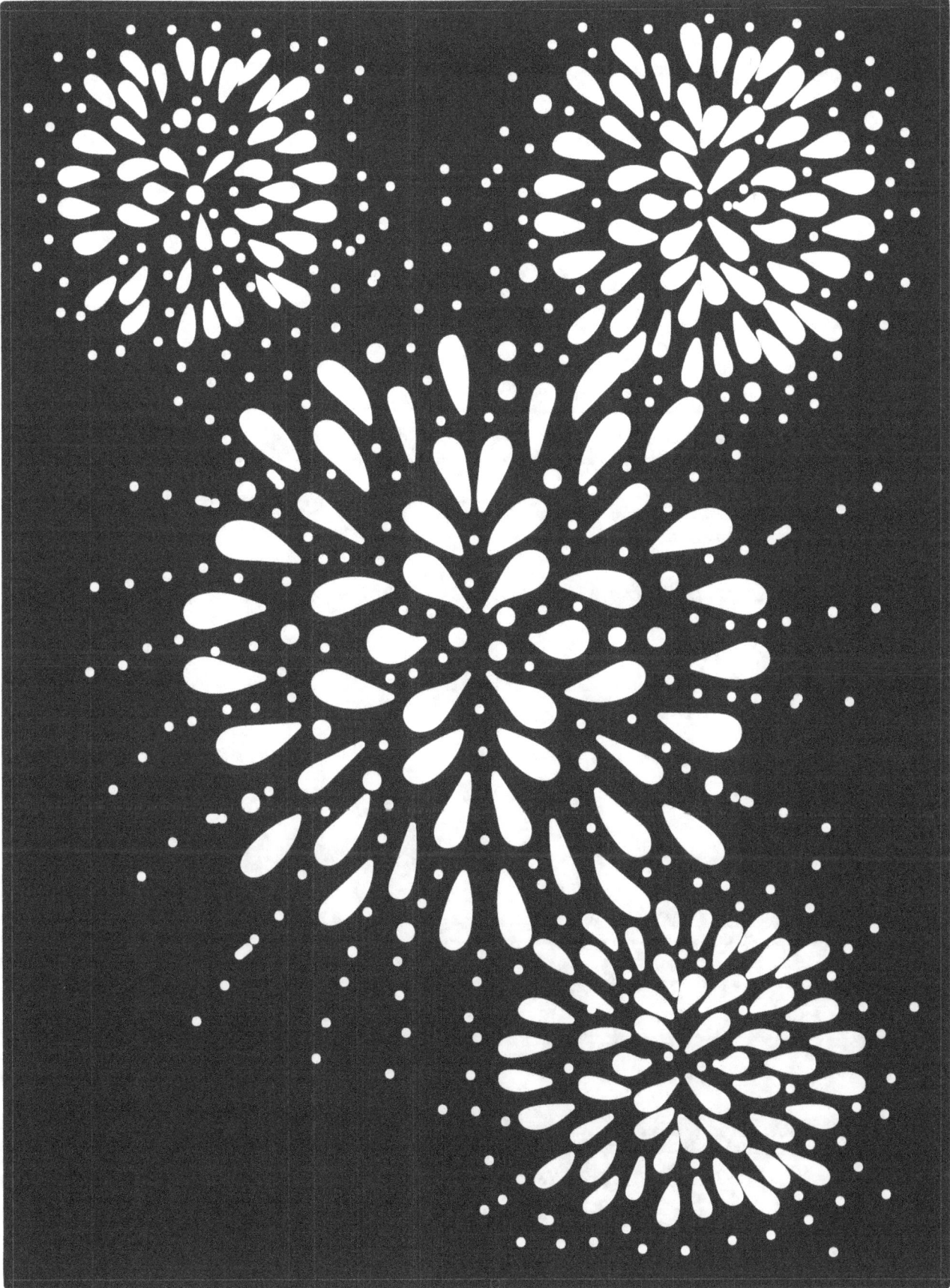

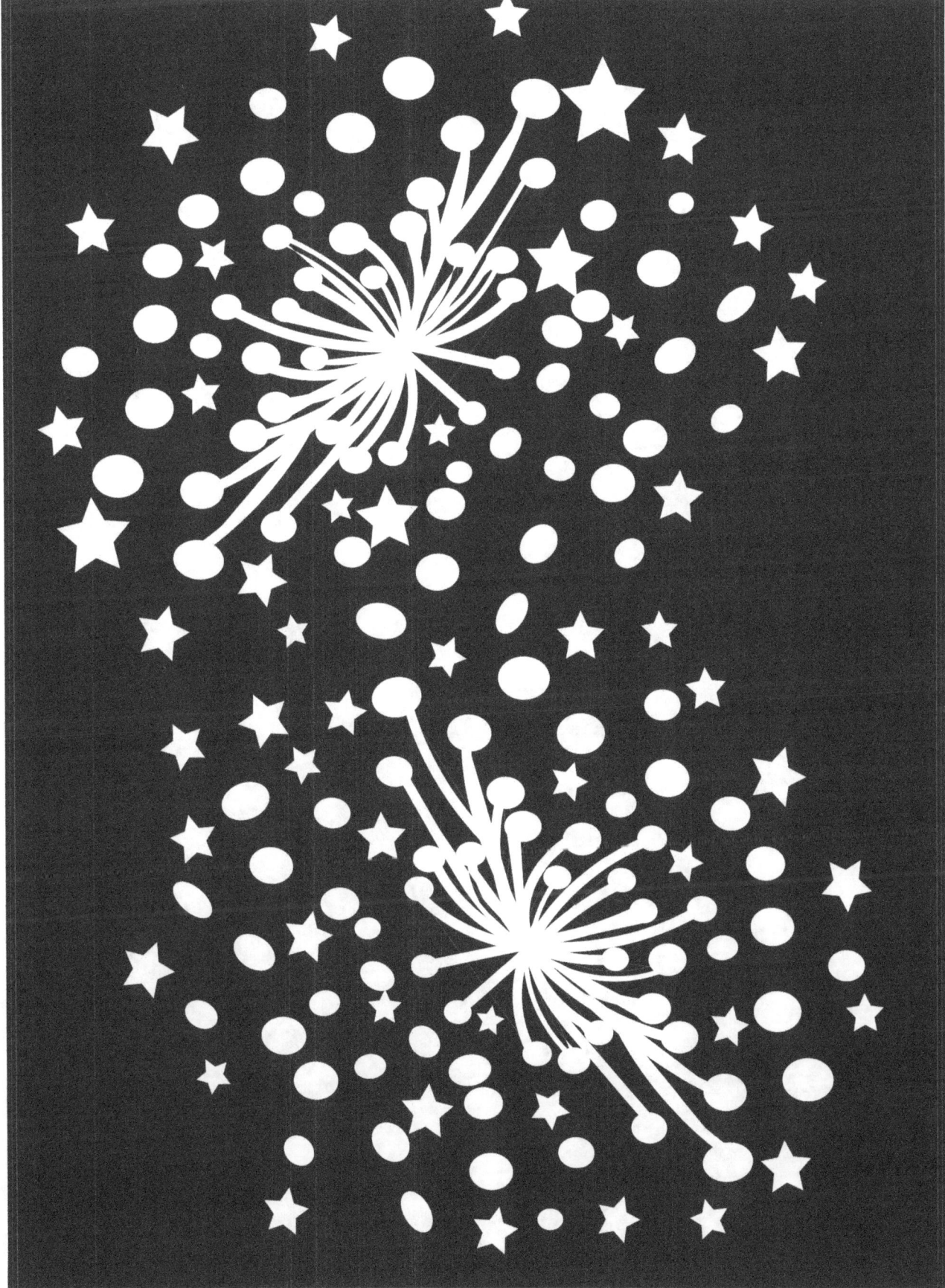

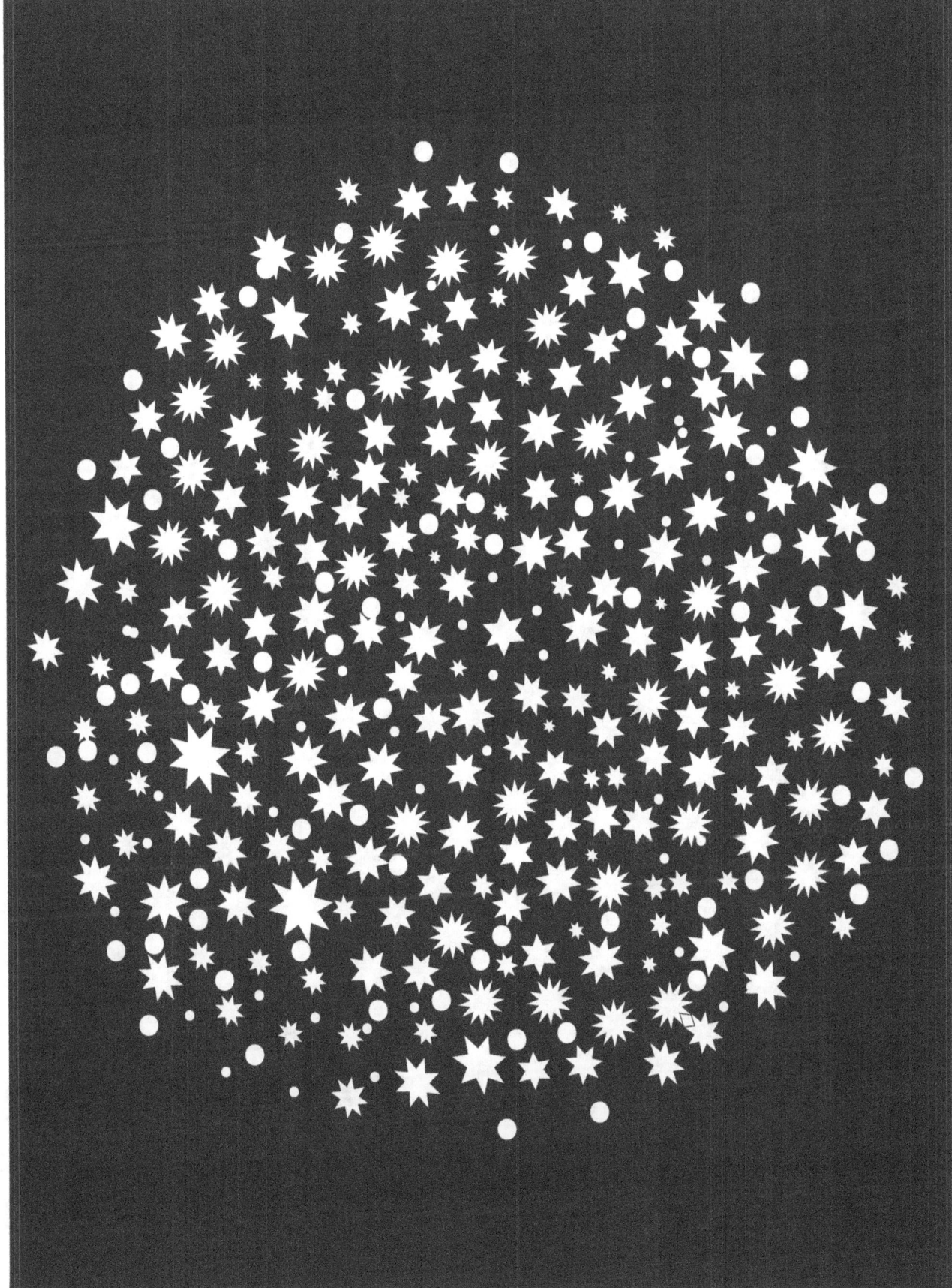

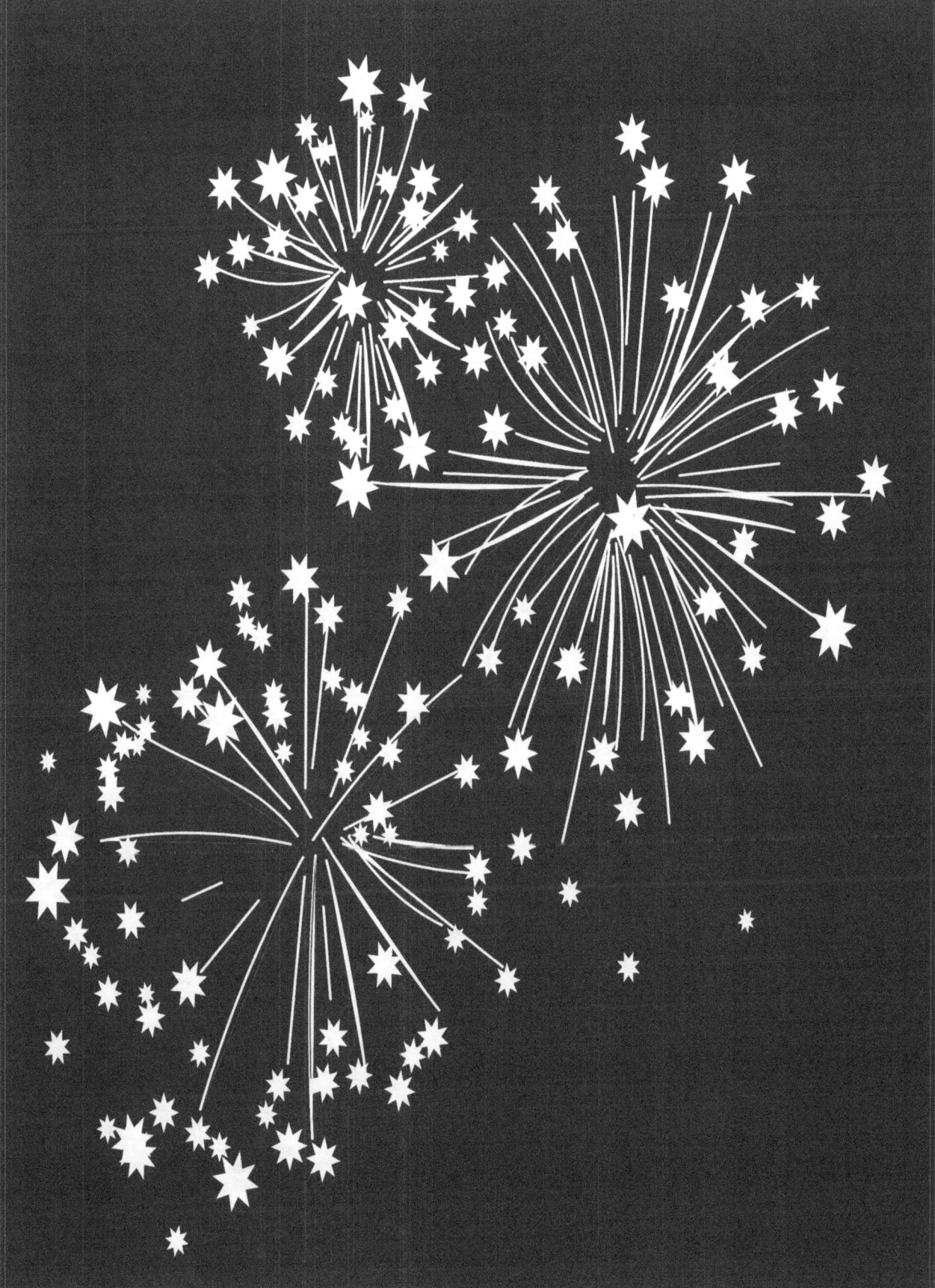

COLOR TEST PAGE

COLOR TEST PAGE

www.ingramcontent.com/pod-product-compliance
Lightning Source LLC
Chambersburg PA
CBHW080001230526
45470CB00008B/2826